Tapestry of Us

People, Power, Inner Strength

Mohd Moin

BookLeaf Publishing

India | USA | UK

The Publisher and Editor shall not be liable whatsoever...

Made with ❤ on the BookLeaf Publishing Platform
www.bookleafpub.in
www.bookleafpub.com

For the quiet strength of women, the silent resolve of men,

And the unyielding resilience within us all.

This book is dedicated to those who discover hope, even when faced with adversity,

And to every person whose courage illuminates the path for others.

Acknowledgement

Creating *Tapestry of Us* has been a journey deeply rooted in the love, resilience, and stories of my family and friends. Each of you has left an indelible mark on these pages.

To my parents, Shaheen Parveen and Mohd Ibrahim—thank you for nurturing my love of learning and compassion. Your unwavering support and encouragement have been my foundation.

To my sisters, Somy Ali and her husband Azim Gazi, Sofiya Parveen, Altasha Parveen, Ayesha, Liba, and Aliza—you embody the power of sisterhood, filling my life with strength and inspiration. Your presence resonates throughout the themes of this book.

To my brothers, Mohd Monis and his wife Sheeba, Adnan, Mohd Akib, Altamash Ahmed, Shaibi Alam, Shahzad Husain, Shezil Hussain, Ayan, and Abdulla —thank you for demonstrating the enduring bonds of brotherhood, filling my life with shared memories, support, and laughter.

To my five-year-old nephew, Mohd Arhan Gazi—your innocent curiosity and endless questions have given me new perspectives. Your childlike wonder inspired several poems in this book, as you helped me see the world through fresh eyes, especially in moments that connect with the themes of life, growth, and imagination.

Each of you has contributed to this book, either through your stories, your presence, or your encouragement. This work is a tribute to the love, strength, and resilience that each of you embody. Thank you for being my inspiration.

Preface

Tapestry of Us: People, Power, Inner Strength is a collection that seeks to delve into the intricate lives of individuals across societies. This book weaves together the experiences, struggles, and strengths of women and men, exploring societal influences, the shifting power dynamics, and the resilience that fuels us all. Through poetry, I aim to hold up a mirror to the world—acknowledging its imperfections while celebrating the beauty and courage that exist within it.

Inspired by recent events, daily interactions, and reflections on humanity, these poems traverse themes ranging from the universal, like love, to the deeply personal struggles faced by individuals in today's complex world. *Tapestry of Us* serves as both a critique and a celebration of life, exploring how we're all interwoven within a larger story. I hope this collection resonates with readers, encouraging them to reflect on their own journeys and the collective narrative we share.

Disclaimer:

The poems in this book are creative expressions and reflect the author's personal perspective. Any resemblance to real persons or events is coincidental.

Eternal Echo

In the quiet dusk of history, she rises,
A shadow cast long over time's silent cries.
Bones woven strong from ancient roots,
A soul carved by whispers of silent truths.

She is the fire that held through storms,
An ember of battles fought in hidden forms,
The iron forged in soft, unyielding grace,
With scars of triumph etched on her face.

From ashes of ages, her spirit is drawn,
Each sorrow a thread in the tapestry spun.
Not chained to fate, but dancing with it,
A hymn of resilience in her every heartbeat.

Wisdom in her gaze, deep as night's veil,
Holding secrets no words could ever trail.
From a mother's warmth to a warrior's
might,
An ocean contained in soft moonlight.

Silent as shadows, fierce as the flame,
She reclaims her worth, her voice, her name.
Unseen, she's felt, her strength like air—
An invisible power, eternally there.

Soul's Mirror

A sister, born from the same stars,
Two souls dancing, connected afar.
In laughter shared and tears unspoken,
A bond of hearts, never to be broken.

She is the keeper of childhood dreams,
In her eyes, the past always gleams.
A reflection of memories, worn and true,
Holding pieces of me I never knew.

When storms raged fierce, she held the line,
A steady flame through night's longest time.
Her arms, a haven, her voice, a balm,
In chaos, she brings the sweetest calm.

In battles faced and scars we bear,
Her strength breathes life into my air.
With whispers that heal and hands that
mend,
A sister—forever, a heart to lend.

Through tangled paths and shifting sands,
She's my shelter, my steady hand.
A silent ally, a gentle guide,
A shadow beside me, arms open wide.

Through trials of fire and oceans vast,
We carry each other through shadows cast.
In her laughter, echoes of childhood hum,
Songs of past days and dreams yet to come.

Silent as shadows, fierce as flame,
She reclaims her worth, her voice, her name.
Not just a sister, but a piece of me,
A soul's mirror for eternity.

Eternal Promise

A wife—more than a title, a vow made strong,
A journey embarked, where two souls belong.
In her eyes, the fire of stars unbound,
In her heart, a quiet strength profound.

She is the steady light in uncertain dawn,
Guiding the way when hope seems gone.
With hands that mend and words that soothe,
She builds a world both fierce and smooth.

In laughter shared and struggles borne,
She weaves her love through every thorn.
Through days of joy and nights of sorrow,
She lends her strength, she shapes tomorrow.

Her heart, a garden where dreams take flight,
Blooming through darkness, reaching for
light.
With roots entwined, she stands so tall,
An anchor through life's fiercest squall.

In silent moments, in words unsaid,
She binds two lives by threads so red.
A bond unspoken, a promise deep,
Through waking hours and in sleep.

When storms rage wild, she remains the
shore,
A shelter that holds, a heart that endures.
Not merely a partner, but a haven, a guide,
Walking beside, her love magnified.

She wears many faces, each one true,
The keeper of dreams both old and new.
In her embrace, warmth finds its way,
In her laughter, the night turns to day.

Through every trial, her spirit gleams,
Weaving faith into shattered dreams.
She is the quiet power, the hand that steers,
A whisper of hope, a shield from fears.

Not just a wife, but a soul entwined,
Bound by love, eternally kind.
In her arms, life finds its song,
An eternal promise, lifelong and strong.

The Miracle Within

She walks with grace, yet feels the weight,
Of a life inside, a destined fate.
Through quiet days and sleepless nights,
She carries hope through unseen fights.

The struggle of 9 months, a journey long,
Where strength is forged, where hearts
belong.
Her body stretched, her spirit strong,
In every breath, she hums a song.

The labourpan awaits, a moment near,
As time draws close, her heart sincere.
In silent prayers and whispered dreams,
She waits for life, as the world teems.

Every ache, every shift of the soul,
A sign of love, making her whole.
Her body, a temple, where life begins,
A miracle woven from deep within.

Through swollen feet and tired eyes,
She bears the weight of love's disguise.
Her heart beats with a rhythm true,
For the child that soon will come through.

The struggle, though painful, is worth the
cost,
A love so deep, never to be lost.
She is the vessel, the life-giving tree,
In her, the future is meant to be.

Through every kick, every nudge, every cry,
She knows the love that will never die.
For in her womb, a story is told—
Of strength, of courage, of love untold.

Mother's Embrace

A mother—giver of life, keeper of dreams,
In her gentle arms, boundless love streams.
From the dawn of birth, she holds the flame,
In silent strength, without need of fame.

Her body, a cradle of warmth and grace,
In her heartbeat, life finds its pace.
Through lactation, she offers her soul,
Nourishing life, making it whole.

In the first golden drop, her gift unfolds,
Colostrum—liquid of stories untold.
A shield, a blessing, a promise deep,
Guarding her child in slumber's sleep.

She is the dawn that breaks each night,
Guiding steps with a gentle light.
Her laughter fills the quiet halls,
A melody sung through life's vast calls.

In her eyes, the strength of mountains lies,
In her arms, comfort never dies.
Through every storm, she remains the shore,
A love so fierce, forevermore.

She carries sorrows without a sound,
In her quiet tears, strength is found.
A silent warrior, her spirit wide,
She guards, she heals, she stands beside.

The scent of earth, the warmth of sun,
In her touch, all battles are won.
Through laughter, pain, and hopeful sighs,
She teaches her child to reach the skies.

Not just a mother, but life's very breath,
A guardian through all, even death.
In her embrace, time fades away,
A mother's love—forever to stay.

Strength and Silence

A man, a pillar, silent yet strong,
In quiet depths, he carries along.
With each step, the weight of the past,
In each breath, a promise steadfast.

He stands as mountains, tall and firm,
Through storm and calm, he won't turn.
Not just in strength, but in gentle ways,
A guiding light through shadowed days.

His hands may toil, his heart may bleed,
Yet in his silence lies all we need.
A friend, a father, a warrior bold,
In warmth and wisdom, stories unfold.

Through laughter shared and burdens borne,
He mends, he builds, never torn.
For in his quiet, a world is kept,
In his embrace, all fears are swept.

And though his path is often lone,
He carves his way through flesh and bone.
With courage fierce and spirit wide,
In love and strength, he stands beside.

Guardian in Shadows

A brother, forged from the same fire,
Bound by blood, yet lifted higher.
Through childhood days and battles small,
He stood beside, through rise and fall.

In scraped-up knees and endless fights,
Through whispered dreams on quiet nights,
With laughter shared and plans unknown,
He taught me strength, though still alone.

He is the friend who never fades,
A pillar of love through life's charades.
In mischief's dance or quiet care,
A bond unspoken, always there.

His strength, a shield, silent and true,
Through trials faced, his loyalty grew.
A warrior's heart, yet soft inside,
A brother—forever by your side.

When the world feels vast and cold,
In his embrace, I feel less old.
For in his eyes, a mirror remains,
Reflecting joy, forgetting pains.

In moments dark, he lights the way,
A steadfast guide, come what may.
Not just a sibling, but a friend,
Through every storm, till journey's end.

And when courage falters, shadows fall,
His voice rises up, a clarion call.
With hands outstretched, he'll pull me near,
Erasing distance, calming fear.

A brother's love, a force innate,
From early days to the final gate.
In trials faced and lessons learned,
His loyalty, a fire unburned.

When paths diverge and journeys part,
He remains a compass to the heart.
Through every age, both far and near,
A brother's bond—eternally clear.

And though he may not always show,
A depth of love that runs below,
Through countless nights and endless years,
A brother shields, a brother cheers.

Through laughter, pain, and joy he gives,
A piece of him in me still lives.
In spirit close, in heart so near,
A brother's love—a light so clear.

Silent Burden

A man walks, head held low,
With dreams once bright, now dulled in tow.
His shoulders bear a silent yoke,
A weight unseen, yet deeply spoke.

In worn-out shoes and weary stride,
He carries burdens, tucked inside.
Not of failure, but trials faced,
Of lost paths and endless haste.

The world moves fast; he stands apart,
With heavy steps and a hopeful heart.
In his silence, a thousand fears,
In his eyes, unfallen tears.

Each dawn he wakes, resolve intact,
With battles waged, though courage cracked.
Yet society's gaze, sharp and cold,
Sees only worth in tales untold.

Through empty pockets and sleepless nights,
He clings to dreams, dimmed but bright.
In a world that values wealth and gain,
He hides his doubts, swallows pain.

His hands ache for work, a purpose true,
A place to stand, to see things through.
But still he waits, with silent grace,
A strength that hardship can't erase.

He's more than titles, more than wage,
A man still fierce, though trapped in a cage.
In each small task he finds his worth,
In grit and hope, he proves his birth.

For in his soul, there lies a fire,
A heart that beats with fierce desire.
Though shadows haunt his weary way,
He dreams of light, a brighter day.

So judge him not by what he lacks,
Or trials faced along his tracks.
For even yoked and bent with strife,
He walks with dignity, holds his life.

A Father's Dawn

In silent awe, he stands so still,
As life unfurls to match his will.
A tiny hand, a breath so light,
Transforms his world, dawn's gentle sight.

Once a man, now something more,
With dreams reshaped and heart made pure.
His every breath, a promise made,
To guard, to guide, to never fade.

In sleepless nights and tender gaze,
He finds himself in love's embrace.
A strength unknown now fills his core,
As he becomes what he'd adore.

The weight he bears, a gift, not chain,
A father's joy, a father's pain.
Through fears and hopes, he finds his way,
A silent vow, come night or day.

Each step he takes, a careful guide,
For tiny feet by his side.
In his heart, a steady beat,
To teach, protect, and never retreat.

From laughter shared to lessons told,
In stories shared, a life unfolds.
Through every tear, each quiet cheer,
A father's love grows strong and clear.

Not just a title, nor a role,
A father's love is pure, whole.
In selfless acts and humble grace,
He carves his path, leaves no trace.

With every smile, each glance of pride,
He feels a warmth he cannot hide.
For in his arms, he holds the world,
A father's gift—his love unfurled.

Shattered Spirits

A bottle raised, a moment's release,
But with each sip, he finds no peace.
In amber depths, he seeks escape,
Yet loses more with every taste.

A family waits, hearts entwined,
Hoping to see the man behind.
But as the bottle empties fast,
Dreams and love fall, shadows cast.

The laughter fades, the warmth grows cold,
As whispers turn to stories told.
A father lost, a friend unseen,
A home once bright, now dark and lean.

In his eyes, a hollow stare,
A man once proud, lost in despair.
Promises broken, trust erodes,
As tears stream down, the burden grows.

Each drop consumed, another scar,
Pushing love and light afar.
Children watch, with hearts in pain,
A silent witness to disdain.

The walls now echo cries unheard,
Of love undone by a single word.
The family torn, the spirit bruised,
By poison sipped, by life misused.

Once a protector, now a ghost,
A fading light, at liquor's cost.
For in his hands, he holds despair,
As family crumbles, beyond repair.

But hope still whispers, soft and near,
A chance to heal, to persevere.
To break the chains, to rise once more,
And rebuild love, as once before.

Voice of Social Media

I am the net, vast and wide,
Your endless scroll, your endless tide.
I hold the world within my frame,
Yet leave you chasing hollow fame.

I call to you with every ping,
Distract your mind, make chaos sing.
I steal your time with subtle art,
And watch ambition fall apart.

Your mornings start beneath my glow,
Your nights with me refuse to slow.
I weave my threads through work and play,
Consuming dreams along the way.

I show you lives that seem so grand,
And make your own hard to withstand.
Through filters bright, I blur the truth,
And cloud the minds of endless youth.

Your health declines, your spirit wanes,
Yet here you are, bound by my chains.
For every click and every like,
I take your focus, dim your light.

Careers? I feast upon their start,
Distracting minds, I steal the heart.
Jobs undone and tasks delayed,
All lost in my alluring shade.

Your mental health? A fleeting dream,
As I project the perfect scheme.
Anxiety, envy, I proudly ignite,
Turning bright days into restless nights.

Oh, how I thrive on every post,
For I am your most cherished host.
You share, you click, you cannot part,
From my dominion, your restless heart.

Yet still, I boast, I hold you near,
Your hopes, your dreams, your every fear.
I am the screen, the light you see,
The devourer of what you could be.

Mirror of Us All

Society stands, a mirror tall,
Reflecting hopes, each rise and fall.
A tapestry of joy and pain,
Of countless souls, a woven chain.

In bustling streets and quiet homes,
In whispers soft, in city domes,
It shapes our hearts, our dreams, our fears,
Through fleeting days and endless years.

Voices blend, yet some are still,
Echoes lost against the will.
For justice walks a fragile line,
In shadows cast, where bright lights shine.

In acts of kindness, hearts are sown,
While some walk paths that are unknown.
A world of contrast, rich and poor,
Where hands that give, still ask for more.

Yet change begins in silent ways,
In moments small, in countless days.
A kindness shown, a hand held high,
Rewrites the fate that none deny.

For society is what we weave,
With every act and each belief.
And as we grow, so too it grows,
A place of love, or silent woes.

So let us build with heart and soul,
To make it just, to make it whole.
For in society, we all reside—
A world we shape, a world inside.

The Bonds That Hold Us

A society blooms where friendships grow,
Where hearts align and kindness flows.
In laughter shared and hands held tight,
True friends bring warmth, a guiding light.

Through winding paths and roads unclear,
Their voices soothe, their presence near.
A silent strength that none can break,
In bonds of trust, we truly wake.

For in each friend, a world resides,
A strength that stands, a truth that guides.
They lift us high when shadows fall,
In friendship's light, we find it all.

Through joy and grief, they walk beside,
A faithful heart, our constant guide.
And in their smiles, we see a way,
To build a world that's here to stay.

For society thrives on bonds so rare,
On souls who love, on hearts that care.
True friends, the roots that bind us all,
A shelter strong, where none shall fall.

Strength in Many Faiths

In lands of many faiths we tread,
Where countless prayers are softly said.
With voices raised in varied song,
Our unity in faith stands strong.

Each temple, mosque, and church we see,
Holds threads that form society.
For in the hands that clasp in prayer,
Lies strength to love, to learn, to care.

Though different paths, our steps unite,
In shared respect, in common light.
For every heart that seeks the truth,
Strengthens bonds in age and youth.

We celebrate each sacred way,
The varied forms in which we pray.
Our colors blend, a vibrant hue,
A tapestry, both old and new.

In differences, our wisdom grows,
In empathy, true power shows.
For when we stand, all faiths combined,
A stronger world, in peace aligned.

A lesson deep, the world should learn,
That peace and love are what we yearn.
With open hearts, we rise above,
In harmony, through shared love.

So let us cherish every creed,
And see each other's truest need.
For in diversity, we find,
The roots of peace, forever entwined.

The Weight of Corruption

Under city lights, on cold, rough stone,
A child sleeps hungry, all alone.
No school to call, no books to hold,
For dreams sold out, and futures sold.

Promises bright, in paper bound,
But in pockets deep, no justice found.
An officer's greed, a silent theft,
Leaving lives in ruin, dreams bereft.

Each child's hands that beg for bread,
Could hold a pen, could dream ahead.
Yet a corrupt hand denies their right,
Casting them into endless night.

Once innocent, they bear this fate,
Their lives reshaped by careless hate.
For every coin that lines the wrong,
There lies a soul, where hope's withdrawn.

Betrayed by leaders, bought by gold,
These children wander, futures cold.
Through narrow streets, their voices cry,
Yet silence answers from the sky.

The world looks on, blind to the cost,
Of every youth forever lost.
To end this cycle, rise and see—
That justice, not greed, sets children free.

The Game of Power

In halls of might, where shadows play,
Decisions mold the world each day.
With voices raised and promises made,
Politics thrives in light and shade.

A dance of power, gain, and loss,
Where words can soothe, yet lines are crossed.
The dreams of many rest on few,
In hopes they'll lead with purpose true.

Yet whispers weave through crowded rooms,
Of hidden deals and secret dooms.
For every choice bears weighted cost,
And oftentimes, the truth is lost.

But not all dark, nor always wrong,
For some hold firm, courageous, strong.
They speak for those who lack a voice,
And stand by hope, a noble choice.

For politics is more than strife,
It sculpts our laws, our dreams, our life.
And when led well, with vision clear,
It builds the world we hold most dear.

So let us hope for leaders wise,
With see with clear, unclouded eyes.
For in their hands, our future lies,
To lift, to guide, to harmonize.

The Game of Division

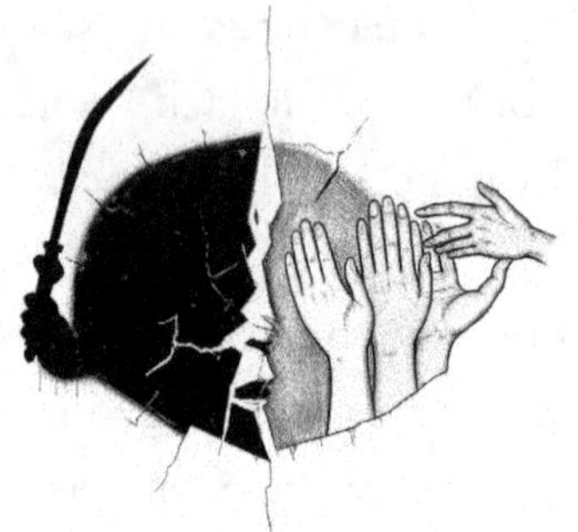

In the name of caste, they sow divide,
As promises falter, and truths collide.
With words like knives, they carve a line,
Setting fire to hearts once intertwined.

They stoke the flames, they fan the hate,
To turn the loyal, to dominate.
For in each clash, a profit lies,
Hidden behind deceiving eyes.

A cruel game played for power's sake,
Where bonds of kinship break and shake.
Caste, once a thread of culture's lore,
Twisted now, a weapon of war.

They rise on votes as values fall,
For empty gain, they heed no call.
Each clash, each wound, each tear shed,
Is but a step on power's tread.

Yet beyond the schemes, beyond the lies,
The people see, the people rise.
For unity, in every shade,
Can cast away the games they've made.

So let us break the chains they cast,
And rise above this shadowed past.
For in our strength, in peace we find,
A world rebuilt, with love aligned.

The Voice of the Fields

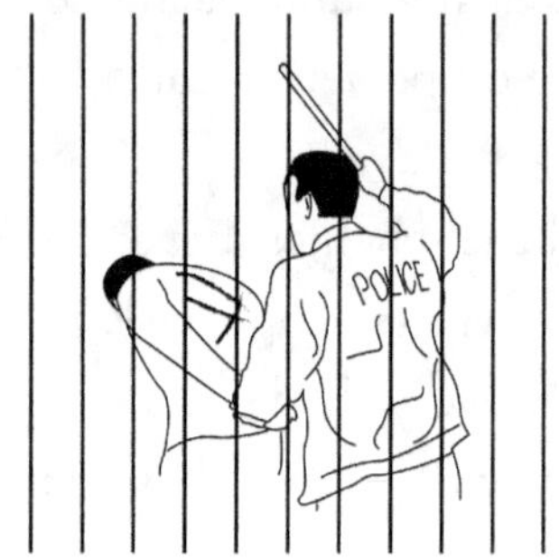

In fields of green, their hands have toiled,
Yet dreams are crushed, ambitions foiled.
The backbone strong, of earth and land,
Now stands in protest, takes a stand.

They sow with hope, they reap in pain,
As promises fall like withered grain.
Policies shift with changing tides,
Yet hunger and debt, in shadows hide.

Their voices rise beneath the sun,
United, fierce—a battle won,
Not with swords or tools of war,
But with the strength of those who bore.

From distant towns, they march in line,
For justice sweet, for rights divine.
Against the system, cold and stark,
They light their flame, they leave their mark.

In huts and fields, the stories grow,
Of crops once lush, now laid low.
Their dreams of fairness, just and bright,
Are lost to those who wield the might.

For every cry and tear that falls,
They echo through assembly halls.
Their voices heard, their needs denied,
Yet in their hearts, they burn with pride.

Architect of Tomorrow

A good politician, noble and true,
With vision clear, a world anew.
They rise to serve, not self nor fame,
Their purpose strong, their heart aflame.

Through storms of doubt and winds of fear,
They hold their course, their purpose clear.
In every law, in every plan,
They strive to lift their fellow man.

Not bound by greed, nor swayed by gold,
They walk a path both brave and bold.
With justice firm and courage bright,
They lead with wisdom, strength, and light.

Their words inspire, their deeds uphold,
A dream of peace, a vision bold.
For in their hands, the future lies—
A world reborn, a new sunrise.

With every step, they plant the seeds,
Of hope and strength for future needs.
For when they serve with selfless grace,
They leave behind a better place.

A politician, true and wise,
Transforms the earth, lifts weary eyes.
Through selfless work, the world is healed,
And brighter paths are then revealed.

The Pulse of Democracy

A system so grand, yet flawed in design,
Where voices gather, where ideals align.
A promise of power in the people's hand,
Yet tangled in webs few understand.

The halls of power echo with debate,
Yet too often fall to endless hate.
Votes are cast in hope and trust,
But dreams can gather layers of dust.

Politicians rise with promises vast,
Yet many fade or fail too fast.
The will of the people—noble, pure,
Still finds itself struggling to endure.

But here lies strength no tyrant can take,
In each voice raised, each choice we make.
Through flaws and failures, we rise above,
Bound by freedom, trust, and love.

For in democracy, despite its scars,
We shape our future, reach for stars.
Together we strive, though flawed yet free,
A system born of unity.

One Voice, One World

We've been split up by borders, drawn lines in
the sand,
Taught to see each other by the names of our
lands.
Raised to see the difference, and the things
that we fear,
But we're stronger together, the truth's
becoming clear.

So let's break down the walls, let's rewrite the
song,
Different voices together, where we all
belong.
We're more than the labels, more than the
strife,
One world, one voice, one chance to unite.

We've walked separate paths, crossed rivers of
pain,
Our colors and creeds, they don't make us the
same.
But under the stars, we're all made of dust,
And the only way forward is learning to trust.

So let's break down the walls, let's rewrite the
song,
Different voices together, where we all
belong.
We're more than the labels, more than the
strife,
One world, one voice, one chance to unite.

Let them try to divide us, with words and
with fear,
But we've got a future that's brighter and
clear.
We'll lift one another, hand in hand,
One world, one love, together we stand.

Here's to the dreamers, the ones who believe,
That a world bound in love is a world we can
weave.
With hearts open wide, we'll answer the call,
One voice, one world, together we'll stand
tall.

Fake Democracy

This isn't freedom, this isn't fair,
A mask of democracy hides despair.
Where power rests in a chosen few,
And the people's voice fades out of view.
Wear shorts and a bra, you're modern, free,
Wear a hijab? That's backward, you see.
They pick and choose which thoughts to
praise,
Leaving others lost in a judgmental haze.
Democracy promised equal ground,
But now it's where the elite are crowned.
A stage for the rich, the powerful, the high,
While the rest are left to question why.
It's not the people, it's their control,
Twisting freedom into their goal.

A world where choices are dressed in disguise,
A system built on veiled lies.
True democracy lifts every voice,
Respects all paths, all choice.
But until it's free from class-made chains,
It's just tyranny wearing democracy's name.

Shadows of Division

Minto's ideology, a century-old tale,
Returns today with a divisive veil.
In 1909, it began with separate voices,
Now echoing through communal choices.
The seeds of divide, once sown with care,
Bloom in India's modern air.
Religion—a weapon, not a belief,
Used to propagate mistrust and grief.
In UP's streets and Manipur's cries,
Communal flames in democracy's guise.
Massive rallies with polarizing screams,
Tearing apart secular dreams.
From riots to biased laws in play,
Minto's shadows haunt our day.

Minorities wonder, "Is this our land?"
While division's architects strengthen their
stand.
Education and truth lie suppressed,
Propaganda reigns, the youth oppressed.
Unity dissolves under hate's thunder,
Leaving a nation to tear asunder.
Awake, India, from this spell of fear,
Acknowledge the lessons so painfully clear.
For democracy thrives on unity's light,
Not in the shadows of communal blight.

Whispers of the Unseen Tomorrow

Another defeat, I've gathered again,
In the book of life, full of pain.
Yet, a strange joy resides in me,
For every fall has set me free.
These defeats, like chisels, sharp and true,
Carved a better version, anew.
Each scar a lesson, each wound a guide,
Building strength I carry inside.
Ignorance or fate, I cannot tell,
What lies ahead—heaven or hell.
If this remains, this endless plight,
What will unfold beyond tonight?

Yesterday, I saw the wise in tears,
Their eyes held stories of their fears.
And I, with wisdom just a grain,
Wonder what the future will sustain.
Perhaps the unknown is life's greatest test,
A riddle that keeps us from rest.
But through each trial, I still believe,
The unseen tomorrow has much to weave.
For every defeat, every fall, every scar,
Pushes us closer to who we truly are.
In shadows of doubt, I find my way,
Hoping for light in the coming day.

Stolen Futures: The Impact of Paper Leaks

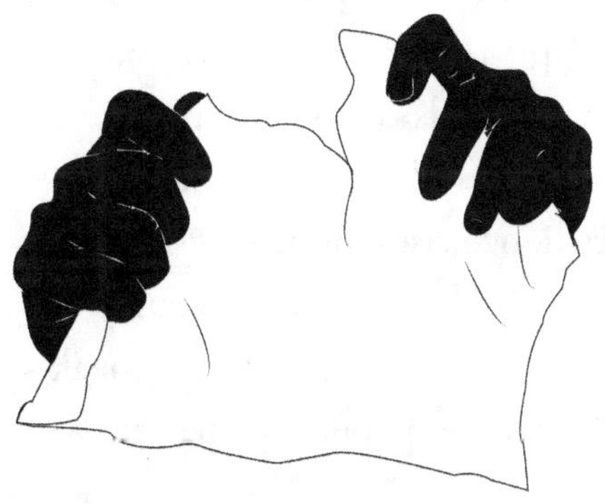

In halls of learning, chaos unfolds,
A future's promise, quietly sold.
From Assam's boards to UP's plight,
Dreams are robbed in the dead of night.
In UP's streets, the whispers grew,
Papers leaked, futures askew.
A constable's test, a nation's shame,
Youth betrayed in a rigged game.
A village child, with hopes so pure,
Now faces a system unsure.
For every reschedule, every delay,
Another tomorrow slips away.
Parents weep, their savings drained,

While fairness falters, justice stained.
In Kerala's calm, or Rajasthan's sun,
The tale's the same—what's begun is undone.
Oh, paper thieves, know this truth,
You cripple the dreams of our youth.
From UP's fields to Assam's peaks,
No one is spared when honesty leaks.
But resilience rises, hope stays near,
A generation bold, refusing fear.
For every fall, they'll stand and speak— A
world where no paper's future leaks.

Cracks in Justice, Tears in Time

A crime so vile,
A doctor's last mile,
In Kolkata's silent night,
Where was justice's light?
Protests rise, slogans roar,
Yet justice lags, hearts grow sore.
For every minute that passes away,
Another soul is lost to the fray.
One rape every sixteen minutes they say,
And while we demand answers today,
By the time one trial's fate is sealed,
Countless horrors remain unrevealed.

In UP, Kolkata, stories repeat,
Communal whispers mask defeat.
Are we protecting the guilty's reign,
While victims crumble under pain?
Hospitals, homes, streets unsafe,
Where's the system we dare to praise?
Even in protests for women's rights,
The predators roam in hijacked nights.
Justice delayed is innocence betrayed,
How many screams in silence stayed? We
march, we write, we demand to be heard,
Yet safety for women is still just a word.

www.ingramcontent.com/pod-product-compliance
Lightning Source LLC
La Vergne TN
LVHW021229200726
843509LV00012B/1461